The Bouquet Talks

The Bouquet Talks

Creations
Patrick Houbrechts & Bea Verbeeck
Sofie Lannoy
Kris De Spiegeleere & Els Van Nedervelde
Anne-France Libert
Bart & Janine Schampheleer

Photography
Isabelle Persyn

stichting
kunstboek

More than words can say...

Without a doubt the bouquet is the most popular gift and a bestseller among floral works. Its name is derived from the French word *bouquet*, meaning a little bunch of flowers, and the wine connotation also hints at those fine scents a bouquet can have. Giving flowers is a special way of communicating. Flowers are messengers, they speak without words.

There are lots of occasions to give a bouquet as a present. You want to thank your best friend? Send her a bouquet. You're visiting a patient so you take a bunch of sunny flowers. For Valentine's day you spoil your beloved with a gorgeous bouquet of red roses. Or you just want to bring spring into your home with a magnificent bundle of tulips… For every event there's a special flower, a typical form, a particular scent, or a combination of these elements.

This book shows creations on the grand themes of love, thankfulness, atmosphere, visiting and farewell. Five master florists – one hundred very different bouquets. Through all seasons of the year, every bouquet tells its own story. You'll discover a whole spectrum of flowers, floral materials, techniques and styles. Moreover, every occasional bouquet is accompanied by an original text. The florists' ideas, the choice of materials and their ways of working with these materials will be a great source of inspiration for other florists. Their creations aim to enjoy and inspire every bouquet lover.

The language of love: Rosa 'Grand Prix' - Galax (leaf) - Ceropegia

Love

Spiny twigs and prickly fruit come together with soft carnations. Sharpness smoothed away.

Carnation Sint Bodega · Rosa 'Sensational' (rose hips) · Brunia laevis · Curcuma (fruit) · Malus · Salal · Quercus · Bacharis 'Magic Star' · Mitsumata (branches)

A romantic biedermeier assembling contrasting materials in the softest tints. Together in good and bad days.

Rosa 'Akito' - Hydrangea arborescens 'Annabelle' - Echinops bannaticus - Nigella Damascena - Eleagnus - Pieris japonica - Senecio Herreianus - Tillandsia usneoides

Deep burgundies, berry
reds and pale pinks get
along in a lovely way.
Shiny leaves meander
through a dense sphere
of heavy rosebuds.
A way to say I love you.

10   Rosa 'Espérance' - Rosa 'Grand Prix' - Asplenium - Rubus fruticosus

A red rose from the heart.
A discrete but intense
declaration of love.

Rosa 'Grand Prix' - Typha - Cornus

Pearly white roses for a newly wed couple.

Rosa 'Avalanche' · Scabiosa · Muehlenbeckia · Vinca minor (branches)

Curvy white lilies and angular dark stalks make a stand. A floral jewel to finish off any wedding dress.

Lilium 'White Heaven' - Asparagus (stalks) - Aspidistra - Steel grass - Ornithogalum

A heart for Valentine's Day.

Rosa 'Grand Prix' · Asclepias 'Moby Dick' · Myrthus · Salal · Muehlenbeckia · Decorative wire

So many years together, as many moods,
as many colours, as many flowers...

*Love is like velvety roses
with little thorny details.*

Rosa 'Tamango' - Rosa 'Black Baccara' - Calla 'Schwarzwalder' - Cosmos atrosanguineus - Coconut - Flexi grass

One regal flower adorns the winter bride.

Phalaenopsis - Senecio (leaf) - Pulp cane - Pearls - Ribbon - Sisal

A bouquet full of glancing eyes...

Chrysanthemum anthimies - Fern Rumora

Twirling twines for every
dance together, knots of
green for every promising
embrace, pink peppercorns
for the spice of love.
Please be my Valentine
today and let's live the
passion these roses speak of.

Different intensities of red, for love is a journey on an uneven road.

Rosa 'Black Baccara' - Rosa 'Grand Prix' - Rosa 'Ruby Red' - Cordeline 'Black Tie'

Two callas, a heart of grass stalks, berries in the colour of love.

Calla 'Renoir' - Sanguisorba officina - Panicum fountain - Viburnum opulus - Hosta - Steel grass - Rubus tricolor

Elegance in full flow…
No reds, but purplish and rosy
tints that show all their glory
and finesse. Immerse your
beloved in the silky luxury
of fabulous flowers.

Calla - Ranunculus - Aspidistra

Two complementary players, the static svelte callas
and the circling grass stalks follow each other's movements.
Perfect harmony, but with a twist.

You make my head spin.

Ornithogalum arabicum - Spathiphyllum - Palm tree (bark) - Coconut - Alocasia amazonica

A whirlpool of slender stalks with curvaceous white callas to walk down the aisle.

Cucumis sativus (fruit) - Calla - Aspidistra - Typha - Phaseolus (tendrils)

Love, passion and warmth. A red heart putting out feelers, a tentative caress of roses and berries.

Rosa Equador 'Leonidas' - Rosa 'Toscanini' - Rosa 'Cézanne' - Celosia Bombay Yellow - Rosa 'Sensational' (rose hips) - Red currants - Quercus

Love is... a posy of red roses.

Panicum 'Warrior' - Rosa 'Baringo' - Viburnum davidii

Elegance in black and coralline: Thymus (branch) · Aspidistra · Calla 'Schwarzwalder' · Dianthus · Steel grass

Thanks

A present of golden callas and roses.
One colour, a thousand friendly messages.

Calla - Rosa - Celosia - Pennisetum - Helleborus (leaves)

One sunflower for mother, safely nestled
in lighter-than-air greenery.

Helianthus annuus · Nigella Damascena (pods) · Eupatorium · Hydrangea arborescens 'Annabelle' · Achillea variety · Coral fern · Rubus tricolor

The warmth and wealth of the callas underlined by various green textures.

Hedera helix (leaves) - Calla 'Red Magic' - Vaccinium (twigs)

A magnificent autumn sunset.

Rosa 'Black Baccara' - Ranunculus - Safari - Anthurium choco - Hibiscus - Ascocenda Suksamran Sunlight - Peppers - Ligularia - Cordyline Black Tie - Coconut - Quercus

The most precious white roses
in between berries and beans.

Decorative beans - Rosa 'Artemis' - Viburnum tinus (berries) - Brunia laevis - Tillandsia usneoides

Large luscious leaves flaunt a variety of the softest petals, buds and rosettes. A pretty piece of proud carnations and luxurious roses.

Anthurium (leaves) · Ornithogalum · Rosa 'Avalanche' · Hydrangea · Rhipsalis · Calla · Dianthus · Brassica

Back from a stroll along the meadows, holding a bunch
of bright yellow and crispy white, she ran into her mother's arms.
Moon daisies for the sun of her life.

A camaïeu of pinkish roses, nuances of sugary tints within an aura of light brown and green circles. Thank you for all your sweetness.

*Just a few flowers, only the softest colours,
but a grand way to show how much you care.*

Rosa 'Talea' - Papaver - Rose fruit - Anthurium midori - Asclepias 'Moby Dick'

A million petals, a rainbow of colours, a never-ending circle that holds many magnificent elements and as much sympathy.

Gypsophila paniculata 'Million Stars' - Dianthus Ivonne - Gerbera red - Craspedia globosa - Rosa 'Peppermint' - Rosa 'Bleu curiosa' - Rosa 'Black Baccara' - Safari - Eustoma russellianum - Gaultheria Shallon - Brunia alodecuroides - Tree fern - Pistachio - Astrantia major - Asclepias 'Moby Dick'

Thank you for lightening up my darker days. Long stems showcase a bundle of gold. Here is the sun to shine on you this time.

Gleichena dicarpa - Helianthus annuus

43

A red sky in the morning. Sunrise is wonderful today. Red bulbs beaming, clouds of green and blue... Thankful for waking up to you.

Tulipa 'Jan Reus' - Skimmia japonica 'Rubella' - Gaultheria Shallon - Myrtus

*Rare dark flowers
with special grey leaves.
A unique combination for
an extraordinary person.*

Scabiosa caucasica - Calocephalus - Fern leaves

Amaryllis, the winter flower par excellence. Icy whites and frosty pinks are embraced by warm sisal fibres. Under the snow…

A winter star with a heart of snowy sparkle. Ranunculus and eucalyptus are the messengers of Yuletide greetings.

Ranunculus - Eucalyptus (fruit) - Aspidistra (leaves)

Zingy, glossy red fruit makes a sweet comfort when summer has finally ended. Blushing callas and roses open up like memories of the beaming summer sun. In between their rays you find a wealth of berries, those little treasures of harvest.
Make hay while the sun shines...

Rosa 'African Dawn' - Rubus fruticosus - Calla 'Red Sox' - Hypericum - Hydrangea - Quercus - Sanguisorba officina - Salal

49

This Christmas, a lasting construction hosts pale pink roses. The red twigs resemble the deathliness of wintertime, the lively apples make a decorative counterpart.

Rosa 'Cézanne' - Calla - Malus - Decorative beans - Rosa 'Sensational' (rose hips) - Peppers - Cornus (branches) - Christmas balls

Glistening pink peppers and velvety black petals peek through a wine-red veil. Roses, cones and conifers say thank you at Christmas.

Rosa 'Black Baccara' - Chamaecyparis - Shinus molle - Pine cones - Angel's hair

Tulip bulbs that are yet to open paired off with ripening berries in a deluge of fern leaves. The ultimate symbol of fecundity, the pomegranate, weds grand callas.

Pomegranate - Calla 'Schwarzwalder' - Tulipa (fruit) - Fern leaves - Rubus fruticosus

*Ivory lilies rhyme
with flamingo flowers.*

Aspidistra - Asclepias 'Moby Dick' - Asparagus setaceus - Chrysanthemum Event - Lilium longiflorum - Lonchocarpus -
Anthurium andreanum 'Maxima verde' - Anthurium andreanum 'Julia'

Mood

The circle of the seasons: Tulipa 'Cheers' - Aspidistra (leaves) - Ranunculus - Steel grass - Woven net

The last days of summer are the brightest and the most precious. Celebrate the season of warmth with the gentle lightness of callas, dahlias and celosias.

A crown of corncobs with bleached leaves enfolds majestic lilies, profuse baby's breath and plenty of white and greenish details.

Eucalyptus citriodora - Eucalyptus cinerea - Lilium longiflorum - Gypsophila paniculata 'Million Stars' - Symphoricarpos - Eustoma russellianum - Zea mais

An airy bunch of ivory tulips heralds early spring.
Nothing but these flowers, a fluff of moss and a hint of wood.
As they grow and bloom, those dark winter nights shorten.

Beautiful days are on the way.
A fresh bouquet because of its
colour and its lightness. Tulips are
the most lovely signs of spring.

Tulipa 'White Dream' - Typha - Aspidistra - Willow

A children's birthday in spring. Playful peppers
and funky gerberas rise and flow in all directions.

Bright pink, childish flowers
and sweet things. Fickle
and playful flowers in a
well-structured arrangement.

Phytolacca americana - Ammi majus - Gerbera - Sweets

Easter: the promise of life. A profusion of tiny eggs and bursting bulbs interspersed with mossy and feathery accents.

Anemone - Tulipa (bulbs) - Olea europea - Salal - Cetraria islandica - Quail eggs - Feathers

Petite bowls of burgundy and rose peek through feathery fern and slender leaves. Spring is in the air.

Ranunculus - Tree fern - Salal

The silver blue of the thistle globes matches
the greyish pink of the Japanese anemone buds.
A moonlit dinner for two on a summer night.

Rosa 'Vendela' · Echinops · Anemone japonica · Ceropegia · Lychen · Palm (bark) · Sisal · Silk thread

The palest pink and the lightest fibre
to welcome a newborn child.

Ranunculus - Ligularia - Sisal

Out of a bed of petals and tiny
apples rise stars of Bethlehem.
They lighten the room from where
their static, immaculate stems
make up a maze. They are
reaching for the sky.

Hydrangea · Malus · Aspidistra · Ornithogalum

How tiny flowers can get gargantuan. A white mass of countless flakes, an avalanche of little suns.

Chrysanthemum 'White Giant' - Gaultheria Shallon

The leafy abundance of summer colours and materials.
A sunny centrepiece at a midsummer party.

Scabiosa Staefa - Allium - Echinops Bamaticus - Limonium 'Happy Wings' - Rosa 'Halloween' - Alchemilla mollis - Quercus - Ligularia - Rubus tricolor - Nigella Damascena (pods) - Daucus carota - Eupatorium - Matracaria - Lavendula - Prunus lutsitanica

Plants become miniature planets –
a cosmos of misty colour and cloudy shapes.

Brunia laevis - Cypress

Sensitive mimosa, sweet buttercups,
lilac anemones, surrounded by
the liveliest greens. It's a gentle
awakening in the sun of the new season.

Ranunculus · Anemone · Rosa 'Blue Curiosa' · Mixed foliage · Lisianthus · Mimosa

*The scarlet glow
of a summer sunset...*

Rosa 'Grand Prix' - Rosa 'Mambo' - Sedum - Viburnum opulus - Parthenocissus - Salal

Bronze callas rise through crushed ribbons of lily-flax.
A collar of rose hips makes every level of this bouquet
equally interesting. An echo of dry autumn leaves outside...

Celebrate the treasures of autumn before winter's austerity.

Corylus avellana (leaves) - Rosa 'Vendela' - Papaver - Peppers - Achillea variety - Daucus Carota - Hypericum - Nigella Damascena - Rubus tricolor - Rubus Chester - Setaria italica - Viburnum tinus (berry) - Prunus (berry)

Around the tree. A warm and colourful Christmas.
A bright mauve for the cold of winter –
a solid fuchsia for warm parties indoors.

From the tiniest volcanoes gush flamy bundles of velvet.
Magmatic black roses bathe in a bittersweet glow.

Rosa 'Black Baccara' - Leucospermum cordifolium - Rosa celastrus scandens - Wood chafing

Indulge in this sumptuous palette of yellows, oranges and reds laced with aubergine and cerise snippets.

Phytolacca americana - Bear grass - Helleborus (leaves) - Datura (fruit) - Amaranthus - Rose hips - Calla 'Schwarzwalder' - Rosa 'Passion' - Rosa 'Marie-Claire' - Anthurium Spirit Antique

An Asian evening: Vanda 'Blue Magic' - Eucalyptus (bark) - Typha - Clematis

Visit

A bouquet flavoured with fuchsia and orange petals inspired by the warmth, the sun and the spices of the Maghreb countries. Tonight we dine in Marrakech...

Rosa 'Bugatti' · Rosa 'Jacaranda' · Dianthus · Phalaenopsis · Ascocenda Suksamran Sunlight · Callicarpa americana · Zanthedeschia 'Red Star' · Anthurium (leaves)

Let the sun shine in any room.

Chrysanthemum Dracula dark - Rosa 'Sunbeam' - Bouvardia 'Royal Roxanne' - Tree fern - Eucalyptus pauciflora - Myrtus - Aeranthos - Gaultheria Shallon

Confronted with the end of summer we cherish every ray of light.
Fluffy lightness as a memory of those golden summer days.

82   Quercus · Castanea sativa · Asclepias 'Moby Dick' · Brunia alopecuroides · Bixa orellana

Lightness and simplicity evoked by an
intricate pattern of endless convolutions...
or how it can take a lot of personal efforts
to achieve peace of mind. Amazon lilies
try to reach the skies and shine their
whiteness on whoever enters the room.
An ideal present at the opening of a spa.

Eucharis grandiflora - Polygonum - Pandanus - Lychen

Static and stately,
lilies rise to a solemn occasion.

Spicy artichoke with garlic
and cranberries. The perfect
bouquet at a barbecue.

Hydrangea arborescens - Sedum spectabile - Allium - Vaccinium - Cynara scolymus -
Sambucus nigra - Rubus Chester - Peppers - Steel grass - Muehlenbeckia

85

A freshly picked bundle to adorn
a picnic with friends.
Green flowers, leaves and grass-stalks
flowing on a summer's breeze.

Soft and sharp, velvety and glossy. A sweet summer bouquet when invited for afternoon tea in a sunlit garden.

Amaranthus - Curcuma - Celosia - Anthurium (leaves) - Steel grass - Rosa 'Cézanne' - Rosa 'Aqua'

Straightforward colours and textures give something to hold on to.

Rosa 'Fabienne' - Dahlia - Physalis - Rose hips - Achillea - Hydrangea (leaves) - Myrtus

A delicate scheme of sober colours.
In the modest beauty of callas, roses and hydrangeas
lays the strength to drive away a melancholic mood.

Hydrangea - Rosa 'Halloween' - Phlox - Astilbe - Sedum - Asparagus - Calla - Photinia (leaves)

A bundle of branches and berries that cherish a delicate circle of tea roses. An indoors Indian summer.

Rosa 'Halloween' - Asparagus - Salix (twigs) - Gaultheria (berries)

A girl is born: Salal - Pittosporum - Hyacinthus - Ranunculus - Ornithogalum - Vaccinium (branches)

White snowberries and green olives bring together purity and peace.
A symbolic bouquet at the baptism of a little child.

Symphoricarpos albus - Olea europea - Pearls

An opening white rose forebodes
many magical moments to come.

Rosa 'Avalanche' - Ceropegia - Viburnum tinus (berries) - Eucalyptus - Eupatorium - Lisianthus - Sedum

*Opening rosebuds in a nest
of feathery veil.*

Rosa 'Mimi Eden' · Anemone · Asclepias 'Moby Dick' · Cotinus 'Royal Purple' · Nigella · Alchemilla mollis · Veronica · Orchid (roots) · Pink feathers · Pink tulle

Stylish chic for an invitation to an elegant party.

*An appealing piece of Victoriana with solemn roses,
airy baby's breath and deep green leaves.*

Hydrangea - Rosa 'Toscanini' - Malus - Peppers - Grevillea - Gypsophila Paniculata

The starting point for journeys
ahead, the foundation that makes
you grow, a niche to cherish…
That's home. The elegance of
a sober, strong basis welcoming
joyful swirls and wine-red drama.

Snowballs and black roses. Juniper berries and frosty green pine. A bouquet that makes rich use of sundry Christmas classics.

Brunia laevis - Rosa 'Black Baccara' - Pinus - Myrtus - Gaultheria Shallon - Juniperus - Nelumbo nicufera - Asclepias 'Moby Dick'- Christmas balls

Tristesse: Tulipa 'Maureen' - Asparagus umbellatus - Cytisus - Asclepias 'Moby Dick' - Eucalyptus - Aspedistra - Rosa 'Avalanche' - Pulp cane

Farewell

An icy net connects dark crooked twigs and white roses.

Rosa 'Akito' - Ornithogalum 'Mount Fugi' - Asclepias 'Moby Dick' - Bacharis - Cordyline - Corylus avellana - Glue nets

The dry roughness of fibres
and branches gives way
to shiny anthuriums.
Light shines into the darkness.

Mossed branches - Agave (fibre) - Anthurium 'Grace White'

A square of dead branches and leaves pedestals solemn whites and purples. Lead ribbons make this an unmoveable memorial.

A flat and long bouquet
adorned with purple orchids.
Though we have to say goodbye,
we'll be connected in beauty.

My love for you, an everburning flame.

Strelitzia - Gerbera mini 'Duende'

Sunny callas and fresh green branches for a gem of a person.

Calla 'Mango' · Cannomois virgata · Parthenocissus · Branches · Grass

Ecosmosis. Fruit and frail roses make our goodbyes unforgettable.

Hypericum androsaemum - Corn fibre - Rosa 'Renate' - Passion fruit (dried) - Pistachio - Myrtus - Lonchocorpus

Drenched in nostalgic colours and dreaming of beautiful moments, I read your letter of goodbye...

Rosa 'Peppermint' - Calla 'Schwarzwalder' - Cosmos atrosanguineus - Cotinus - Eucalyptus (bark) - Coconut - Pandanus

Three of the reddest roses joined tight together. There is only my love for you... yesterday, today and tomorrow.

Saying goodbye...
Food for meditation

In the springtime
of your life,
you parted from us.

Moss branches - Aspidistra - Narcissus - Cytisus (branches) - Iron wire

Entangled in love,
we'll defeat death.

Calla aethiopica 'Highwood' - Codyline (leaf) - Typha

Roses in a moonshine colour,
imbedded in a hopeful green orb.

Hydrangea macrophylla - Rosa 'Peppermint' - Anthurium andreanum - Pistachio - Tree fern - Leucadendron - Bixa orellana

The sun shines, flowers bloom,
but this silence will always remain...

Chrysanthemum 'Figebri' - Eucalyptus polyanthemos - Tree fern

A refined bouquet of orchids. A torch of flowers, beads and grass that lightens the memory of you.

*Luminous buds
of Rosa 'Espérance'
give a spark of hope...*

Calla 'Schwarzwalder' - Pomegranate - Rosa 'Espérance' - Agave

Who's who?

Domus Florum

Janine and Bart Schampheleer
Molenstraat 45
B-9300 Aalst (Belgium)
info@domusflorum.be

An eyecatcher of Domus Florum is
the 'bouquet of the day', a composition
inspired by the daily supply of fresh flowers.
Their favourites are roses, seasonal flowers
and natural materials.

Fleur d'Ô

Anne-France Libert
Louis Thysstraat 6
B-1150 Sint-Pieters-Woluwe (Belgium)
fleurdo@belgacom.net

In Anne-France's small flower shop, cut
flowers call the tune. She adores bouquets
and has a special feeling for colour schemes.
Her favourites are spring flowers (ranunculus,
muscari, tulips etc.) and roses, callas,
amaryllis, eucharis – noble flowers in general.

Monet

Patrick Houbrechts and Bea Verbeeck
Motstraat 6
B-3570 Alken (Belgium)
monet@telenet.be

At Monet's you'll find ready-made bouquets,
but more often they work according to the
customers' wishes. Patrick likes romantic
bouquets. He doesn't have a favourite
flower – he loves them all.

Palladio

Kris De Spiegeleere and Els Van Nederlvelde
Werfstraat 1 & Blankenbergsesteenweg 279
B-8000 Brugge (Belgium)

Kris and Els love modern floral compositions;
their bouquets are always built around certain
tints of colour. They particularly love sober and
stylish symplicity.

PhiloSofie

Sofie Lannoy
Stationsstraat 44
B-8830 Gits (Belgium)
haven-lannoy@telenet.be

Sofie doesn't like your everyday kind of
flowers. She developed a very own bouquet
style that is feminine and light. She has
a distinct preference for ranunculus,
anemone, asclepias and daucas carota.

Creations

Patrick Houbrechts & Bea Verbeeck (Monet): p. 19, 29, 42, 43, 44, 53, 57, 67, 69, 76, 81, 82, 99, 100-1, 106, 108, 111, 114, 115

Sofie Lannoy (PhiloSofie): p. 2, 8, 9, 22, 28, 33, 36, 45, 50, 60, 61, 68, 73, 84, 85, 95, 96, 97, 102, 103, 104

Kris De Spiegeleere & Els Van Nedervelde (Palladio): p. 10, 13, 20, 23, 24-5, 27, 30-1, 32, 34, 37, 47, 52, 54-5, 63, 66, 72, 77, 88, 92, 112, 113, 117

Anne-France Libert (Fleur d'Ô): p. 11, 17, 21, 26, 35, 40, 41, 46, 59, 64, 65, 74-5, 78-9, 80, 83, 86-7, 105, 109, 110, 116

Bart & Janine Schampheleer (Domus Florum): p. 4, 6-7, 12, 14-5, 16, 18, 38-9, 48-9, 51, 56, 58, 62, 70, 71, 89, 90, 91, 93, 94, 98, 107

Photography

Isabelle Persyn

Final editing

Mieke Dumon

An Theunynck

Layout & photogravure

Graphic Group Van Damme, Oostkamp (BE)

Printed by

Graphic Group Van Damme, Oostkamp (BE)

Published by

Stichting Kunstboek bvba

Legeweg 165

B-8020 Oostkamp

Belgium

Tel. +32 50 46 19 10

Fax +32 50 46 19 18

info@stichtingkunstboek.com

www.stichtingkunstboek.com

ISBN-10 90-5856-190-9

ISBN-13 978-90-5856-190-9

D/2006/6407/10

NUR 421